TURKISH
HANDMADE CARPETS

A. NACİ EREN

HİTİT COLOR
KARTPOSTAL SANAYİ TİCARET VE PAZARLAMA LİMİTED ŞİRKETİ
Cağaloğlu yokuşu, Çele Han No.39 İstanbul Tel: 526 56 51 Fax: 520 78 49

Art Selection and Design: MELİH ÖNDÜN
Graphic works: SERDAR TOPOĞRAF
Photographs: CEMAL MERMER, MEHMET AVCIDIRLAR, MELİH ÖNDÜN
Translation: HELEN ATAKAN
Color Separation, montage and prints:
Typesetting: ÇINAR FOTODİZGİ

ISBN 975-7487-26-0

Special thanks for the contribution of ŞENGÖR HALICILIK in the
preparation of this book.

ABOUT THE AUTHOR

A. NACİ EREN

1932   Born at Göynük, BOLU
1939-51 Finishing the first and secondary schools, he graduated from the Teachers Training School of Edirne
1951-54 Studentship on Painting at the "Institude of Gazi Eğitim" in Ankara
1954-65 Teaching, Art History and Painting at Military College of Merzifon, Kahramanmaraş and Erzincan Highschools.
1965   He began to work as Reseracher at the Museum of Antalya
1965-86 Ethnographical researches at Antalya Museum, restoration of the "Atatürk's House" at Salonica, earning "The Rector of Culture" degree, working as Second director of the Antalya Museum.
1986   He died in Ankara

He earned an extraordinary ethnographic treasure to the Museum oo Antalya and to humanity in his twenty attentive and sistematic years of his life.

Some of his works are: Yörük Göç'ü (Nomads), Kara Çadır (Nomad Tents), Döşemealtı halıları (Carpets of Döşemealtı region), Çoraplar (Turkish Socks), Yörük Çuvalları (Namads sacks), Kaşık ve Kaşıkçılık (Turkish handmade spoons and Spoonmaking), Deri ve Dericilik (Leather and Leathercrafts), Antalya Müzesi Mezar taşları (Epitaphs of Antalya Museum), and the other many unprinted researches..

CONTENTS

Until today many things about carpeting have been published. During the last years publication of this kind have increased immensely. Eventhough there are numereous publications, there are no more than three pieces which can be called "book". These books are: "The ancient and modern Turkish Carpeting and a World Carpet Panorama" by General Kazım Dirik (publ. 1938), "The Seldjuk Carpets" by Oktay Aslanapa and Yusuf Durul, and "The Art of Turkish Carpeting" by Şerare Yetkin.

It is essential to say that publications other than these, made for touristic and commercial reasons, have been very inneficient in offering any remedy to the problems carpeting is facing.

The information given here, -especially in the historical partis nothing more than a mere repetion of what has been said until this day. But for the purpose of contributing something new, this book will try to give the phases of sheep shearing, raw wool turning into yar n and how this turns out to be a carpet when it comes out of the loom.

And again some problems of Turkish Carpeting have been discussed briefly. Also, opinions of foreign researchers and scientist and some special characteristics of the carpet weawing centers of Anatolia will be included in this book.

It must be very clear that this publication has been realized with very limited references and possibilities.

Anatolia still has a vast culture of "hand-woven carpets". It is necessary to add immediately that this culture has been very much degenerated within a very short changing process in some of the weaving centers. So it is necessary to find out all of the weaving centers and to examine them thoroughly down to the smallest detail in order not to loose track of the diminishing carpeting culture.

As Yusuf durul has pointed out, rather than teaching weaving to the weaving centres a new(yarn, design and coloring included) it is necessary to learn weaving from them. We believe that starting out a reserach based on this principle will be very helpfull to the "Turkish Weaving Art".

ABOUT THE CARPET

Reasearches done up to know show us that 'Halı' (carpet) is a Turkish word. The former pronounciation was 'kalı' which means 'it won't wear out, it will last long.' Maybe the word kalı also stood for 'the personal goods of the bride.'

In his book "The antique and modern Turkish Carpeting and the panorama of World Carpets" General Kâzım Dirik gives us the following information:

"B.Ali Sami, who died while he was a member of parliament tells these things about some of the researches he has done in Iran. The persian pronounciation of the word 'halı' is "kalı". But this word never appears in old persian books .The Persian themselves accept this fact. But this word can be easily found in old Turkish dictionaries. Since carpets are somewhat thicker than kilims they must have used the word 'kalın' (thick). And with time this has changed into 'kalı' and 'halı'.

In the arabic language there is no word that matches the word 'halı'. According to the Islamic Encyclopedia the name has derived from the name of a town where big carpets were woven. This place was called Kalikala (Erzurum) In his book called "An Introduction to Turkish Culture III" Professor Dr. Bahaeddin Ögel says that nobody saw the words kalı or halı in sources dated before the XVIth century.

"In the Dede Korkut book, where there are some dialogues with the highland Turks there is a sentence which goes: 'ala kalı ipek döşenmiş idi' (the multicolored kalı was made of silk). Since the Dede Korkut book is a source which contains the oldest Turkish and middle-east traditions it cannot be imagined that a word of foreign origin would be used in such an important mythological piece. So it would be wiser to look to search for Turkish rather than persian or arabic root for the word 'halı'.

Again according to Prof.Dr. Bahaeddin Ögel in his book "An Introduction to Turkish Culture IV: "In the Uygur era the thick and rough materials were called kalıngöz (kalın bez) which means thick cloth. This supports the doctrine of B.Ali Sami who says that "The thing which is thicker (kalın) than the kilim, has changed into halı or kalı with time.

Although there are many different ideas about the motherland of the carpet many scientists agree on the Middle-East.

According to some, carpets were first woven in Kalikala (Erzurum). As a source they show Hamaian Yakut's "Mü'cemülbuldan" and Ibn Havkal's "El-memalik ve 'Imesalik". But actually in neither of these scripts is there a any record about this subject. Some believe that the motherland of the carpet is Iran although the Iranians themselves do not accept this. Kurt Zipper says that: "The more researches on ancient history are intensified the more it is believed that the Middle-East which is the motherland of the Turks is also the motherland of the carpet. Kurt Erdman says: The motherland of the carpet is the whole west side of Asia which lies between 30 and 45° meridian. 'And he adds that this textile which would gain immense importance in the future has developed in Turkish regions.

In her article which was published in the "Turkish Folklore Researches" magazine, Macide Gönül says: "According to Riegl, the carpets produced in the with the nomad knotting style, can be seen in earlier times since carpeting of the nomads is one of the oldest popular arts. So this art remained in a very pure way and it is produced for reasons

Avunya-Manastır, Arşın Çeyrek (20th Cent.) 1.14x1.47m., 3x3 knots per cm², wool.

such as hand, tent, floor and ornamental usage. The origin of this knotting technique should be searched among the people who were the ancestors of the nomads."

Şerare Yetkin, in her book "The Art of Turkish Carpeting" says: The discovery of this technique is based on the simple fact that the nomads needed a thicker and more warm keeping ground." Assistant Professor Dr. M.Kemal Özergin says: "The carpet which is a product of the nomad handcrafts and arts turned out to be a very useful thing for their life-style."

Nejat Diyarbekirli in his work "The Hun Art" shortly says that : "Starting from the earliest ages, the sheep have been one of the most important commercial factors after the horse in eastern Turkish tribes........................... Since the Turkish tribes were the most typical nomads thoughts that they would be very important in production should only be accepted naturally. Many scientsits agree on this idea. So it can be concluded that carpeting was a present from the Turkish to the modern civilizations."

Accepting that the motherland of the carpet is the middle-eastern parts of Turkish areas and that the word halı is of Turkish origin should only be natural since researches about carpeting support these ideas.

Eventhough at the end they all turn out to be the same definitions are all expressed

differently. Kenan Özbel defines the carpet as: some sort of weaving which is brought about by adding more frequent and stronger knots in order to be able to ornament it more easily. Thus the carpet is a knotted and fluffy weaving which is ornamented with various designs on the surface. In the Meydan Larousse Encyclopedia it is defined as: A beaded and/or knotted thing to spread and it is made of wool or silk and it is used either to hang on the wall or to put on some furniture. General Kâzım Dirik the carpet as a thickening of the kilim which are woven in accrosswise manner. They are made of wool or of cotton. Or he says that it can be defined as a surface made of yarn which is knotted on two vertical and one horizontal thread. Oktay Arslanapa and Yusuf Durul in their book "Seldjuk Carpets" define the carpet as a beaded or knotted various covers in different sizes, whose surface is ornamented with various designs and is used for the purpose of spreding on the floor or on furniture or for hanging up the wall. In "Turkish Encyclopedia" the carpet is defined as a fluffy and embroidered weaving. Nowadays we can see single colored carpets with no designs. But we can recognize the carpets which we classify according to country, region and date by their traditional designs. So, because the design is very impartant it should have its place in the definition of the carpet. So according to this the carpet can be defined as a weaving of various sizes, woven for various reasons and that are knotted embroidered and fluffy.

An exact date for when the carpet has first started to be woven cannot be given. And the dates which are given are only mere estimations. The oldest carpet that is found is in the Pazirik-Iskit tomb. It's 1.89x2.00 cm. in size and woven with the Gördes knot with a brilliant technique and it dates back as far as the 5-3. centures B.C. In the Turfan excavations, carpets of the 3rd and 6th centuries A.D. have been found. Then there is a long time gap until the 13th century. There are 18 Anatolian and Seldjuk carpets of which eight are in the Konya-Alaeddin Mosque, three in the Beyşehir-Eşrefoğlu

Mosque and seven in Mısır-Fustat. But one of the carpets in the Beyşehir-Eşrefoğlu Mosque is now lost.

Some sources report that the thirteenth century Konya carpets were the best of their kind. For example Marco Polo remarks that the most beautiful carpets were woven in Anatolian cities like Konya, Kayseri and Sivas.

"A traveller like Marco Polo who has been to Iran and seen the Persian carpets as well couldn't have qualified the Konya carpets as the most beautiful. Eventhough the gorgeousness of the designs and colors and their archaic size could affect today's person they couldn't have affected a Venetian businessman of the thirteenth century. So there must have been much more gorgeous carpets than the ones woven in Konya and even Iran. The carpet mentioned must heve been woven for the Seldjuk Palace. The Konya carpets onthe contrary were woven for everyday needs. Up until now none of the line woven Seldjuk carpets could have been found." Kurt Erdman says that Rudolf M.Riefstahl has these things above in 1931. As a result he agrees with Riefstahl and continues "The best is to believe in Marco Polo's opinion. The Konya carpets were really the best of the thirteenth century.

Again Kurt Erdman gives the following information to support the ideas above:

"Another proof that support Marco Polo's ideas is the information given by Ebul Nida who refers to Sa'ide who died in 1274 (The turcoman carpets which were exported to all countries were woven there) and the weaving center was Aksaray. Ibni Batuda who travelled in Anatolia praises the carpets which were exported from Aksaray to Egypt, Syria, Irak, India, China and Iran."

In is obvious that these carpets which were classified as the most beautiful in the world could not have achieved this much success during a very short period of time. So according to this must have stared to weave not after they came to Anatolia but they must have started earlier when they are in Horasan. Because all the people that came to Anatolia were not all wanderers but some were half-wanderers and some had settled

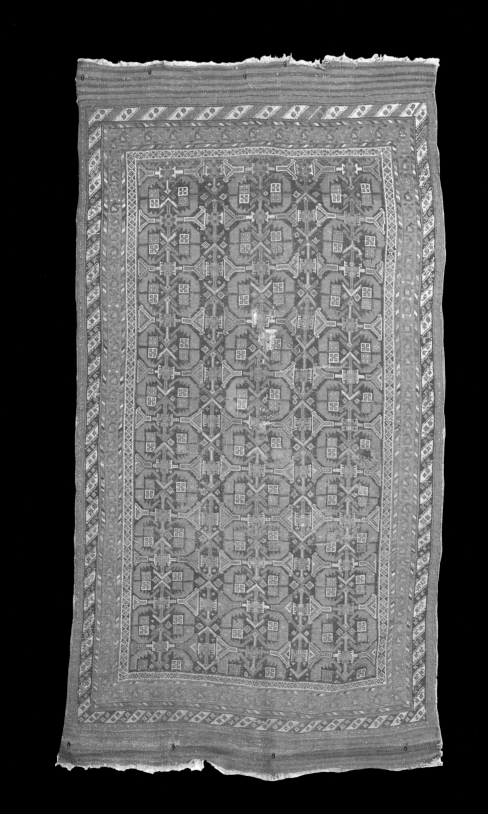

Yahyalı (20th Cent.) 1.34x1.86m., 4x4 knots per cm² wool.

for good. But still the thirteenth century Seldjuk carpets were the highlights of this weaving art. Designs which were created after the principle of eternity, written brodures and the wonderful harmony of the designs were an inspiration of the "Şemse" design on the Koran.

By turning the medaillons into stars the starred carpets were obtained.

The main figures which give the name to the 'birded Ushaks' do resemble birds although they are a touch of floral figures.

In the skin designed ones, the base is filled with clouds or with small dots.

The compositions of floral designed and Chinese designed carpets are very similar. The designs are made of two big rectangles which are filled with round figures that resemble flowers and clouds.

In these types it seems as if the base designs would go on, continue even after the bordures. This shows us how much the weavers have stuck to the 'principle of eternity'.

The eighteenth century is a time when the Turkish carpet remained close to its tradition and characteristic. As it is known the eighteenth century is a timewhere great change and corruption in all important arts is seen. But the carpet whose roots have been strong, resisted this corruption and it did try to do so even in the ninteenth century. Among the factors which have affected our carpets, especially in the big centers, the influence of persian carpets and european arts could be ranked in first place. It is because of these in fluences that there has been a decrease in demand for our carpets.

On the other hand there are quite a number of centers which could be strong enough to stay pure. The Bergama-

Yuntdağı region is one of these. The carpet called 'tabaklı' has geometrical designs which date back to the fifteenth cent. So we can see how strong the tradition is.

It can enver be claimed that any art has come about without any influences or that it has just suddenly popped up. But this influence has to be molded with creativity and the national identity. Heinrich Glück explains this very nicely:

"Whenever the Turks went to a new country the same thing was alwasy repeated; they used to work on the local arts but they put their own spirit into it. Other than this the Turks would take back with them the artists of the countries which they had seized and thus they combined the foreign art with that of their or they have just accepted it as their own art." But since the Turks are the first ones to weave a carpet and since it is them who have turned carpeting into an art and science the last part of the observation above cannot be accepted.

One of the big and important carpet groups in the seventeenth and eighteenth centures are the prayer rugs. Among the important centers are Kula, Gördes, Ladik, Bergama, Milas, Mucur, Kırşehir etc. The prayer rug is actually woven in all centers of Anatolia.

In the nineteenth century Hereke shows itsself as an entirely new type of carpet. In 1891 the carpet department was added to the Hereke factory which was established in 1844. Nurettin Yalman gives us the following information:

"Skilled foremen were brought from Gördes and Demirci to the new opened carpeting department in 1891. These foremen were trained for some time at the looms in Istanbul which were making carpets for the palace and thus the typical and special carpets of Hereke have been started to be woven. Among these the 'Gobelin type' carpets are the most interesting ones.

The twentieth century is a time when the corruption of the Turkish carpet has intensified. The factors causing this corruption are design exchanges between centers, synthetic dyes, and the yarn and knot problems. And although we can add change into naturalism with the influence of the persian carpet we must add that there are still some cecnters in Anatolia which weave carpets that are as beautiful as the old ones.

The republican era should be considered as a time when serious studies heve been started. And the last years show a big increase inte studies of this kind. It would be better to continue these studies for the middle-east Turkish regions since these regions are the orgion of the carpet and since carpeting wasn't introduced in Anatolia before the Turkish tribes immigrated there. In these studies priority shouyd be given to kilim, sili, cicim and sumak which are plain weavings and another priority should be the newly establishing carpet weaving centers. This would be very heypful to the tribe and village weavings. It would do no harm to try to make use of the design studies because the centers could make use of the designs by using them as long as the design belongs to the region itself and as long as this is done consciously. As Kurt Zipper says: "Turkey is a very rich country in terms of its rugs such as kilim, sili and cicim. This such a richness which no other country can copete with.

If the thirteenth century carpets are examined closely it will be seen that they show a very big resemblence to those of the fourteenth and fifteenth century ones. Usually the same designs were used and both era carpets put a lot of importance into geometryzation and style and of these the latter still shows a big richness in Anatolia. Some of the regional names of the designs are 'çömlekçi (potter), deve boynuzu (camel horn), dokuz göbek (nine middles), zobusu, dana gözü (calf's eye), tomasu, boncuksu, çakmak, etlik, bütün alabalığı (whole trout), koç boynuzu (ram's horn), göbekli yanış, karakıvrım, karabudak, göklü, elibelinde, pıtrak, bulanık, sığır sidiği (ox'es urine), sekiz köşeli yıldızlar, (eight cornered stars), toplar (balls), kırık ayna (broken mirror), ayna kırığı (a piece of a broken mirror), ağaç ve dal motifleri (tree and branch designs). These designs which were used in the thirteenth, fourteenth and fifteenth centuries were still used in the eighteenth century although with some amount of decrease.

The same situation con be observed in today's carpet as well. So according to this, the need for researching these kinds of plain weaving shows itself in a natural way . But this richness is facing a period of diminishment so a quick study and research should be done in order to be able to fit it into today's culture.

There are some researchers who believe that the origin of some of the designs should be searched in old Turkish beliefs. Since the same sort of designs can be seen on different kinds of pieces of art this idea seem very acceptable.

In his book "The Hun Arts" Nejat Diyarbekirli says the following:

"Because the Sky God Ülgen was the symbol of goodness, a small number of horses were sacrificed for him. But the people who tried to protect themselves from the underground gods sacrificed a large number of rams and mountain sheep, plus they put many rams and mountain sheep miniatures among their belongings in order to save themselves and their belongings as well.

Another design which was used as much as the ram's horn,was the muska (talisman). It is triangular in shape and it must have descended from the tripple belief. The tripple belief reresents the threegods (Sky-Sun-Fire) of the ancient. Turks and it also represents the three powers of Allah (creation-letting survive -taking away life), after the acceptance of Islam. Abdulkadir says the following.

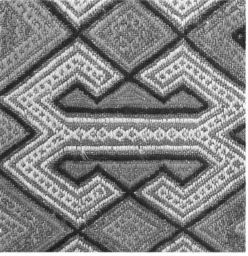

"During the years, the Kutadgu Bilig was written by the Turks who started to accept the Islam and naturally they must have realized the necessity of getting adapted to this new religion. So drive away the devils they have used talismen on which prayers were written".

Another design which is very often seen on carpets is the 'çakmak' (lighter) design and this can be related to the fire cult. "In the Ataic and Yakut tribes fire obtained from flintstone was very sacred." Later it was discovered that fire could be obtained from iron and flintstone. The important thing here is the name. The sparkling was done by a

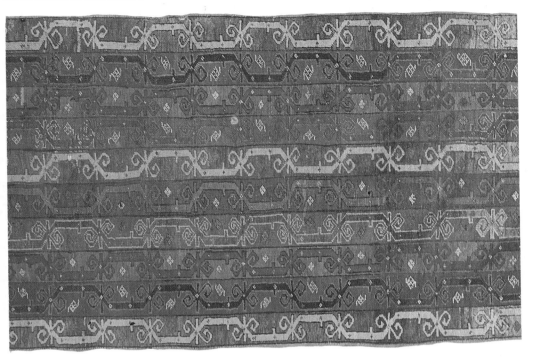

Kırşehir-Mucur, Yolluk (20th Cent.) 1.15x2.60 cm. 4x4 knots per cm², wool.

tool made of iron, so the shape of this iron tool has a great deal of importance for us. On many carpets the 'lighter' design can be seen in various forms.

By ornamenting the foursame triangles which are obtained from folding-in the corners of a square or a rectangle we get adesign, which in some sources is referred to Tai-Ki. This design, nowadays is called the 'kırık ayna' (broken mirror) or 'ayna kırığı' (a piece of broken mirror) in some regions. This design is made up of the two parts of a round figure divided into two. One part is dark the other is light. This symbolizes darkness and light. Thes same sort of symbolization is used in the stone and iron art works of the Anatolian Seldjuks. And usually lion, eagle and dragon figures were used as symbols.

The design which is called the 'branch' and 'tree' design is related with total masses of trees and it can be said that this symbolizes 'The Tree of Life".

Although there have been many changes in the designs, the colorsand composition of carpets we don't see a change in plain weavings. This kind of weaving has carried on with all of its tradition.

Inspite of some technical differences plain weavings like kilim, sili, cicim and sumak, show great resemblence with hand woven carpets; in color in design and in composition. So the transition from plain weaving to carpet has been a very easy and appropriate one. The reason for this is that, these designs which don't apply to painting are in fact very suitable for the characteristic of the carpet.

So we can say that the Turkish carpet was at its peak in purity and tradition in the thirteenth, fourteenth and fifteenth centuries but that starting on the sixteenth century it was influenced by elements seen on tiles, embroideries and architectural works. It is necessary to reapeat that the medaillons seen on sixteenth century Ushak carpets

◁ Caucasian-Divanlık (20th Cent.) 1.42x2.8 m. Wool. 3x3 knots per cm².

19

have been imitations of the decorative figures of the sun.. And again niches, colons and chandeliers all have been sources of influence. These various designs should be considered as a natural result of the Turkish genius and creativity, harmonized with the carpet characteristic.

Although the creators and the mother-land of the carpet are Turkish we see that the persians have a larger export market, when observed from an economical angle. Though there are many reasons for this is the main one is that the studies which were started one century ago used the persian carpet as a starting point instead of the Turkish one. Kurt Erdman claims that the Persian Art is totally based on miniature and adds the following:

"Pictures and rugs have seperate rules and they don't combine together... The Turkish carpet has never shown a close relation to the miniatures like the persian does. Because of this the development has been more consistant. Because the factors which have been supporting the carpet were strong and forcefull the carpet has survived the through the forcase around it. Even nowadays some carpets which show the beauty of the ancient ones, are made in Anatolia.

We would like to mention some of the opinions of foreign scientists and researchers such as Kurt Erdman.

J. Stryyzgowski: ".......... The world famous Seldjuk Carpets should be discriminated from the eastern carpets which were presented to the Seldjuk ruler as a gift, by the governments under the reign of the Seldjuks. Marko Polo says that the best carpets were woven there and that silk of dark red and of other colors were woven as well. When talking previously about Zemarchos'es and Dizabol's tents he refers to the same subject."

Dr. Hawley (Oriental rugs, Antique and Modern):

"The colors of the Anatolian carpets are usually brighter than those of the Persian, Indian and Middle-eastern ones. Even-though red, blue and yellow were not used very brightly their harmony was much better than those of the Chinese and Caucasian ones.

There is also a difference in picture other than in color. In Anatolian carpets there is much more art than the others... The figures used as design had meaning and harmony as well as the harmony in colors.

There is averyelaborated art in Anatolian carpets, especially in prayerrugs. The reason of this is that the residents of Anatolia had a much more superior sense of religion and art."

Th.Gauthier has made notes about this during on a trip to Istanbul in the middle of the ninteenth century. About his visit in the Bazaar he says:

"The foreign woolen clothes which had to bright and biting colors and which were embroidered with silver thread were only there to emphasize the beauty of the oriental taste. These exported clothes created such a blunder that I couldn't keep myself from gnashing my teeth. I hate and blame the industry which brings these ugly colors and uses them as trade goods, for they do disturb the harmonious taste of this place."

General Kasım Dirik quotes these words from Prof. Riefstahl in one of his conferences:

"The most beautiful and antique Turkish carpets are existant in Anatolia. But to track down their dates, era and that room which they were woven in is a very tough job, even for a scientist. But thanks to the Turks and to civilization we can find out the dates of some of the carpets by examining the gifts given to the Venetian churches. By comparing those in the treasury with those in Anatolia we can estimate their almost exact date an value. And of course not to mention that at those times the most valuable present which could be given was the Turkish carpet and rug."

I think it would be suitable to close this part with the words of Kurt Zipper: "We still hope that the Turkish nation will defend its cultural inheritance and that it will not prefer the foreign and deceitful beauty symbols to that of its own; an art which it has created within itsself. Because the foreign art threatens its own with death. The Turkish carpet which has an honorable past will continue its fame and value."

MATERIAL AND TECHNIC

It is known that the raw material of the carpet is wool and that wool is obtained from sheep. Sheep are shorn twice a year, once in spring and once in fall. The one shorn in spring is called 'yapağı' and the one shor in fall is called 'yün'. The fibers of the yapağı are longer, more contiguous and dirtier whereas the fibres of the yün are shorter, further apart and cleaner.

The shearing scissors are called 'kırklık'. The kırklık is made up of three parts; two iron parts that make up the scissors part and a piece of wood that holds the two iron handles together. Its length is usually 35-36 cms. The with is 2.5-3 cms in the widest part. The handle length is 12 cms and the lenght of the wooden piece is 5-6 cm. (1).

The shorn wool is dried after washed. After it's dried the wool is combed in order to get rid of any waste or anything else that might still be in the wool. The wool-combs are made of iron and wood. The wooden part is called'oturak tahtası' and it is 55-60 cm long and 15-20 cms wide. There are usually two rows of iron teeth which are 11-13 cms long. This comb may also be called 'kıl tarağı' in some parts of Antalya. As seen in (III. 2) it can also be made in various shapes at the Bergama (Pergamum) region.

The combed wool, which is in bundles, is then put in a tool called hallaç' or "yay' (bow) and the fibres are seperated there. But because the fibres of the yapağı (spring wool) are too long they cannot be seperated by the help of a bow. So this process is done by hand instead. (III. 3)

This yay is made of a piece of tree that bends toward the end, a bowstring and wooden support which is fastened to the backside of the tree. This part is called 'yay çenesi' (bow jaw) in some regions. The bow is 160-170 cms long and the jaw is about 25-30 cms. The bowstring is made of sheep or cattle intestines. The bow has other tools to it. These are called 'İlahat' or 'Atacak' (thrower)-a tool which at both ends has pestles- and the 'Çıbık' a short thin piece of tree. The bow string is hit with the thrower so that the fibres can be seperated. The çıbık serves to hit the wool. (III. 4)

CARPETMAKING TOOLS

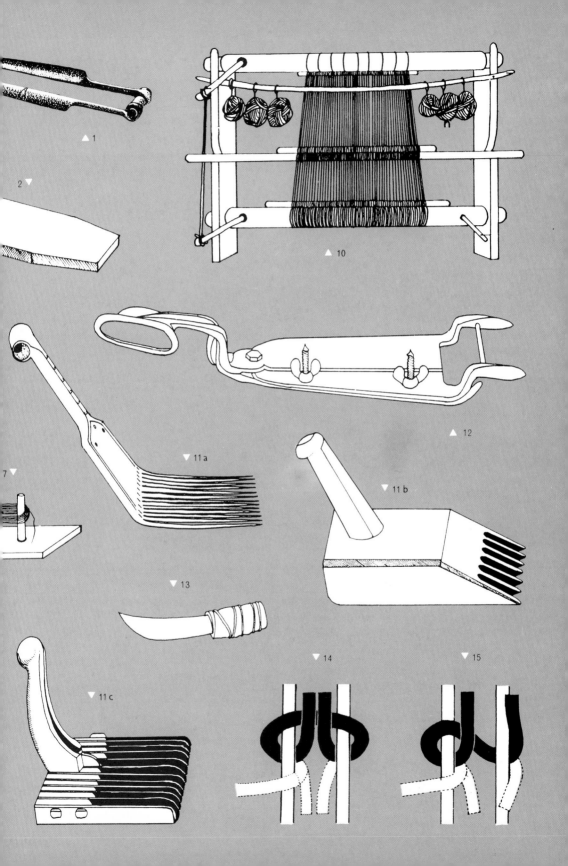

After this process the wool is spun with a wooden spindle called the 'kirman' and then finally it turns into yarn.

The kirman is usually made up of two parts: a) the kirman arrow and b) the kirman wings. As known, one of the wings intersects the other one at the middle. In some cases it is seen that an extra piece called 'ağırşak' is added to the kirman. The length of the arrow is 25-30 cms long. (Ill. 5). In the Antalya-Gündoğmuş region other names for the kirman are 'Tengere' or 'Tengerek'.

'Iğ' or 'Teşi' is made of two pieces: a) the arrow and b) the spindle whorl. The same tool is called the 'Eliği' (hand spindle). If the spindle whorl is placed at the top instead of the bottom of the arrow then it is called 'tengirek' by the nomads of Antalya. The length of the arrow is 30 or 40 cms. The diameter of the whorl is about 5,6 or 7 cms. (Ill. 7).

The tool which helps the spun yarn to turn into a measure is called 'Ilgıdır'. The ılgıdır consists of two parts: a) the streching trees (of which there are two) and b) The wooden pedestal on which the streching trees are placed. The pedestal is about 60-65 cms long and 20-25 cms wide. The yarn bunch which is coiled around the streching trees is called 'Gülep' or 'Kelep' (Ill. 8).

The 'Teçce' or 'Çark' or 'Çıkrık' (spinning wheel) is made of two tools tied together. The Kelep is coiled around this tool. The spinning wheel is made up of a wooden wheel and through the top and the bottom of this wheel and a pedestal, intersects an axle. The height of the wheel is usually 50 cms and the bottom width is about 20-25 cms (Ill. 9). The spinning serves the purpose of spinning a doublelayer-yarn and turning this yarn into a bobin.

Carpets, kilims, rugs and other weavings are all woven in a loom called 'Istar'. This loom is made of two vertical and two horizontal trees. The sizes change according to the material to be woven. Average measures for the vertical trees are 160-170 and 220 cms for the horizontal ones. (Ill. 10)

The verticaltrees are called the 'Istar Dikmeler' in almost all the regions and the horizontalones are called 'Alt ve Üst Oklar' (the upper and lower arrows) in Antalya. The vertical tree in the middle is the 'Gücü'. The tree above the gücü is called the 'Varandinae tree'. The stick under the upper arrow is called 'üst çubuk' (upper stick) in Antalya, 'çomber' in Adana and 'baş yastık değneği' in Milas. The bottom one is called 'çözgü çubuğu' in Antalya, 'askı ağacı in Adana, and 'alt yastık değneği'in Milas. The trees that reach out to the right and the left of the upper and lower arrows are called 'sıkma ağacı' (squeezing tree) or 'sıkma kolları' (squeezing tree) or 'sıkma kolları' (squeezing arms) or 'gerdirme kolları' (streching arms). The handle which is made of iron or wood and which is placed to the right of the lower arrow is called 'Burağ kolu' or 'çevirme kolu' (turning handle) in Antalya and 'sarma demiri' (coiling iron) or 'sarma kolu' (coiling handle) in Milas.

Other tools which are used during the weaving process are: the wool knife, the scissors and the 'kirkit'.

The kirkit is used after a row of knots is finished and the woof is pulled through. The kirkit is used to hit both the knot and the woof in order to squeeze them. And to make kirkits usually the wood of olive trees, boxtrees and mulberry trees was preferred because they were stronger and harder than the other trees. The wooden kirkit does not rumble the wool. The avarage measures for this kirkit would be 8x15 (for its base) and a height of 15-20 cms. (Ill. 11) Nowadays iron kirkits are used as well. These are either made of solid iron or they are made both of iron and wood. (Ill. 11 b c)

The scissors are a special designed tool which cut the edges of the knots in a regular way after the row of knots has been finished. It is also called the carpet machine, carpet scissors or 'sindi'. It is approximately 28-30 cms. long. (Ill 12)

The knot knife is small. Behind a piece of cloth is wrapped so that it can serve as a handle and also that it does not hurt the hand. It is approximately 12-13 cms. long. (Ill.13)

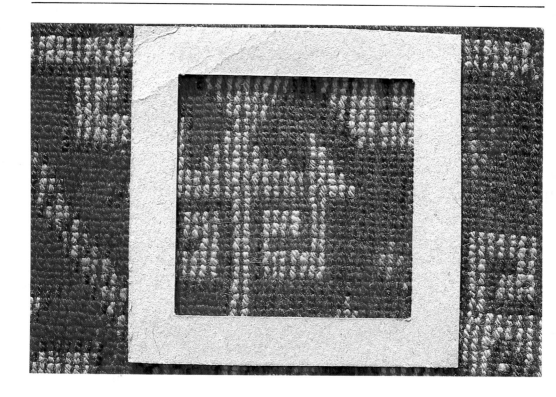

In order to be able to weave a carpet three kinds of yarn have to be produced by the wooden spindle.

1) Çözgü yarns: These determine the skeleton, in other words the strength of the carpet. So they must be produced in a very tight and thin way. They are also called 'eriş' or 'arış'. They are vertical yarns.

2) Atkı yarns: They are produced less tightly than the çözgü yarns. They are called argaç (woof) and they are horizontal yarns.

3) Knot yarns: These are the least tightly produced yarns.

To start the weaving process, first of all the çözgü yarns have to be streched out on the loom. This process is done somewhere else and it is called 'çözgülerin çözülmesi' (the untieing of the yarns)

To do this, two wooden (or iron) stakes which are chosen according to the measures of the carpet, are nailed. Beside each stake there is one person and there is someone else between the stakes. One end of the çözgü yarn is is tied to one of the stakes and the yarn is then streched out to the other stake. The person in the middle sees to it that the yarn goes back and forth from one stake to the other. The person by the stake makes a double knot after each second turn. The number of this system is determined according to the width of the carpet to be woven. In the Antalya-Döşemealtı region the measure is taken like this: the numbers are 6x40, 7x40 or 8x40 and then these are turned into length measures such as 6.40, 7.40, 6.40. After the yarn has been coiled and tied around the stakes, the upper stick and the çözgü stick are passed through the çözgü yarn and the upper stick is attached to the upper arrow and the çözgü stick is attached to the lower arrow. Small holes have been carved into

the arrows at the part where they are going to be attached to the sticks. Both in the upper and lower arrows six, seven or eight holes have been carved beforehand. So the arrows and the sticks can be attached together very firmly and by the help of the streching (or squeezing) arms they will be streched very much.

In Turkish carpets there is one loop for two çözgüs. This kind of knot is called 'Gördes' or the 'Turkish Knot'. For this kind of loop (as seen in III.14, the yarn first goes around the front and the round the back of the first çözgü and then again round the front and then round the back of the second çözgü. After this the ends of the yarn are pulled down and the loop is squeezed. The 'Sine' in other words 'Persian Knot' (III.15) is almost the same as the Turkish one except that the yarn only goes round the back of the second çözgü and then it is not pulled down but instead it stays up.

After one row of knots is finished usually two woofs are passed through. Both sides, where the woofs make turns, are called 'kıyı' (edge) or 'kıyı kolanı', 'kenar' (side) or 'etlik'. One row of knots is called the 'sıyırdım'. The number of rows vary according to the çözgü measure system. For example in the 6x40 system there are 120 knots, in the 7x40 system there are 140 knots and in a 8x40 system there are 160 knots. In the Bergama-Yağcıbedir region there are 100 knots in a small rug and 400 knots in a bigger one.

The yarns that hang loose from the shorter side of the carpet are called 'saçak' (string). The borcades show a very special characteristic in nomad and tribal carpets. The strings are long, they are either beaded or they are unbeaded but they have a knot at the end. In the ancient rugs there were four or more rows of these beads. But the modern ones have only one or two rows.

The bead and string part are followed by the 'kilim' part. This part serves to prevent the wearing out and loosening of the carpet. The ornamented part that surrounds the carpet like a frame is called 'bordür' (bordure). The wider one is called the 'enli bordür' (wide bordure) The one inside the wide bordure is called 'iç dar' (inner narrow) and the one outside the wide one is the 'dış

dar' (outer narrow bordure). These bordures are important in the sense that they show the characteristics of their regions.

The section within the bordures is called the 'zemin' (base)

In some carpets in the very middle of the base there is a very big design that is called 'göbek' (center). The triangular spaces which appear at the four corners and are between the center and the inner narrow bordures are called 'köşe' (corner) and they are usually ornamented.

Carpets can be divided into three categories such as:

1) Ground Carpets 2) Rugs (proyer-rugs) 3) Carpets woven for various reasons.

The ground carpets have many base designs although they are woven in large measures. These are made for floor usage but of course there are carpet woven in smaller sizes also for floor usage. So the first category should acctually be called 'Carpets for floor usage'.

The rugs can be collected under two categories a) One-piece rugs and b) upre rugs.

The pure prayer rugs are made for mosques. So they are numerous and they are put side by side in the mosque.

The one-piece-rugs consist, like the other carpets, of one piece. These can also be categorized in two, a) with niches or b) without niches. The carpets with niches can be divided into groups a) single niched b) double-niched c) staired-niche d) plain niche.

The ancient rugs have single and plain niches. At the top parts of some prayer rugs there are some designs. These are called 'ayetlik' (place to read verse) The same design may be at the bottom sometimes. Then it is called ayaklık (pedal).

The figures a prayer rug is ornamented with, are usually oil-lamps, niches chandeliers, mosques, trees, tomb-stones, geometrical and floral designs.

The ones in the third categories, as the name implies are made for various reasons such as for the usage of roads, walls, door, pillows, bags, saddles and saddle-bags. And their names change according to the place they are used.

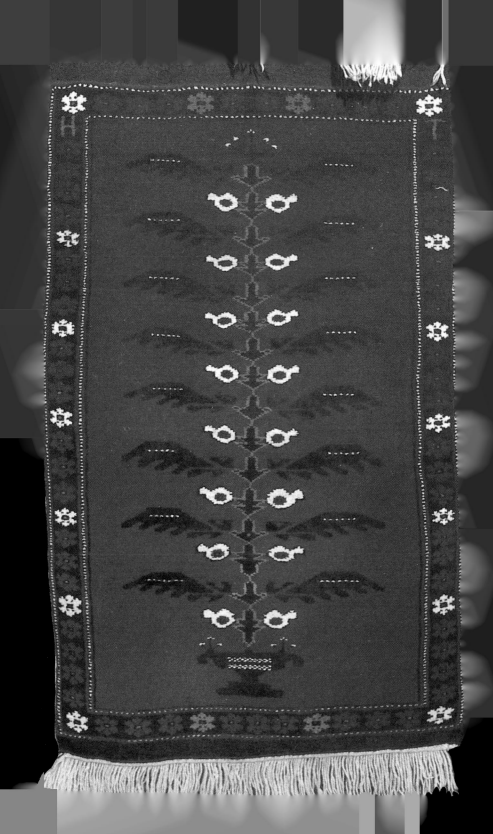

DYES

One of the most important factors that made the Turkish carpet valuable was that the dye was totally vegetal and the colors were very harmonious. It has been observed that until 80-90 years ago the dye used in carpets was one hundred percent vegetal. After that synthetic dye came into use in Anatolia. But there still are some weaving centers which continue the old tradition of using vegetal dye in carpets. One important thing that should be emphasized about dye is that aside its beauty it must be risistant to water, light and friction.

The dye obtained from various parts of various plants are called 'kökboyalar (rubiales) and the act of dying is 'kök-boyacılık'.

The plants which these rubiales have been obtained from for centuries all grow in Anatolia. It is also known that, in Turkish carpeting, the color red is very important. This color and its various tones are obtained from the 'kökboya' (madder tree).

The importance of the color red can be explained by old Turkish beliefs about the fire cult.

On the other hand, blue is also a color used very much in Turkish carpeting. All sorts of blue, varying from dark blue to light blue, are used.

The Sky God Ulgen that represents goodness and kindness is best symbolized with the color blue. This might also expain why evil-eye charm (nazarlık) is blue. But nowadays the usage of red and blue can rather be explained in aesthetic terms.

It is not possible to search and examine all the plants from which the dye is obtained and how the deye is applied according to different weaving centers. Because of this only the Milas and Antalya-Döşemealtı regions will be given as examples.

In Milas The roots of the madder and the agnus castus, the crusts of acorn and wallnut-are used. The ones used in the Antalya-Döşemealtı region are spurge, leaves of the agnus castus, vine leaves, Patience-dock roots, pomegrenade crust, the leaves and the crust of the wallnut tree and are used. Very rarely in XX the Döşemealtı region the leaves of shaff, mulberry and tomato as well as the onion shells are used. Madder roots, sumac gallnut, and oak tree are some of the plants which have been forgotten in the Döşemealtı region.

Milas (20th Cent.) 1.10x1.76 m. 3x3 knots per cm2, wool.

MILAS:

Red: Obtained from the roots of the madder. These are collected during summertime. They are washed and dried in the sun and then they are pulverized in a mortar. The yarn is boiled together with this pulver dye. Forreach measure of yarn one spoonful of lemon salt and one spoonful of alum are added. The yarn is washed until it takes the red color and then it is taken out and dried.

Tones of red and brown: To obtain brown and red-brown color the same process which is done for the red color is repeated. Then after the yarn is taken out it is dipped into ashes and dried under the sun. After it is dry it is rinsed with cold water and then dried again.

Light pink: The yarn is put into the water of the madder which has been boiled a few times and has lost its color. The yarn is boiled with this light colored water and then pink is obtained.

Camel hair: Camel hair or light brown are obtained from the acorn tree. The pulver of the acorn can be bought in stores. The yarn and the pulver go throught the same process as the red-color-process.

If wallnut crust is boiled with alum then a darker tone of camel hair is obtained.

Green: The yarn is boiled with the branch and leaf and root of the agnus castus. After the yarn takes the color the agnus castus is taken out and turquoise is added. The yarn is reboiled and it is taken out when its color turns into green.

Yellow is obtained from agnus castus and alum.

To obtain black agnus castus, stamp dye and package dye are mixed together. The yarn is boiled until it turns black and then it is taken out washed and hung to dry.

ANTALYA-DÖŞEMEALTI

In the Antalya region the yarn goes through two processes in order to be dyed. In the first one the yarn goes into direct process with the plant. This is called 'ipin acılanması' (bittering of the yarn) of 'ipin kestirilmesi'.

Until very recently gall nut and acorn were bittered into black, red and dark blue. For this process the above mentioned plants are dried and then pulverized. The yarn to be dyed is boiled with this powder. Then it is taken out and dried. The dried yarn is then put into an earthenware pot. This is the second process. The pot contains a mixture which has been prepared beforehand. This mixture is composed of water with ashes, animal urine, 'siyek' (the waste collected from between the legs of the sheep) and synthetic dye.

Pomegrenade crust, and sumac are among the colors which are bittered for red and black.

Plants used for bittering into green are vine leaves, spurge and ezentere. The process for them all is more or less the same.

Adding 50 grs. of alum for each kilo of yarn, the yarn is boiled with the plant until it takes the color of the plant. Then it is put into another caldron which is filled with ashed water. The yarn is boiled in this solution until the water gets warm. The yarn stays in this ashed water for about one day. Then it is taken out and washed with cold water. After that it is put into an earthenware pot that contains a mixture composed of indigo-dye, powder of patience-duck root and lemon juice. Together with the yellow colored yarn white colored yarn is put into that mixture, too. The white yarn takes the takes the blue of the indigo-dye.

Some regions obtain a color with the help of patience-duck root in only one process. The patience-duck root is used in two ways. It's either pulverized or just rubbed and put into the cauldron. Together with the pulver alum, lemonsalt, sour plum juice and red synthetic dye is added. This mixturi is boiled in water. The yearn is put into this boiling solution and it continues to boil for 15 or 20 more minutes. After the solution cools off the yarn is taken out, dried and finally it is washed.

To obtain red some green is added to this mixture. The amount of green depends on the darkness wished to obtain.

To obtain red from the madder the root of the madder are dried in the shade. Then they are pulverized. Water which contains some amount of camel waste and a small amount of acorn crust powder, is boiled in a cauldron. The water is not heated up to the boiling point. It is rather preferred warm. Then tye and this warm water is sprinkled on the yarn and then the yarn is rubbed. After that the yarn is put into an empty basin and then it is boiled in water, only. Next it is rinsed with ashed water and then hung up to dry.

Sometimes a weaver can run out of a specific color of yarn whereas the part which should have been woven in that specific color has not been finished yet. So another set of yarn is dyed again but the second outcome may show a slight difference in tone. But anyway that part of the carpet is woven with the other color yarn. This is called 'abrajlı'. In the Milas region this is called 'aperejli'.

In carpets the knot frequency is determined by the numberof knots in each cm^2 or dm^2. The number of knots can be counted from the backside of the carpet.

In some regions, the design which is drawn in milimetrical measures, is hung on the loom, to a place where it can be easily seen by the weaver. These milimetrical designs are prepared to make it easier for the weaver. These miniature designs are called 'sample Paper'. In nomad origined weaving centers this kind of sample paper is not used. The weavers there weave with a very masterful skill.

The quality of a carpet depends on the design, composition, color harmony, dye, knot and yarn. And of course the quality of weaving cannot be forgotten.

Since carpets are an art of weaving the desigh should be in association with the weaving character and should represent the weaving characteristic of thet region.

Antalya-Döşemealtı (20th Cent.) 1.31x1.83 m. Wool. 3x3 knots per cm².

The ideal yarn for carpets are the yarns which are spun by the kirman. The yarn fibres spun with the kirman are both long lasting and long in length. In machine yarn one should pay attention that the fibres are spun as long as the ones on the kirman. It is said in some regions, short fibred-yarn which is mixed with artificial yarn, has started to come into use. Yarn which is mixed with artificial fibres, doesn't absorb the dye very well so this leads to short lasting dye and as a result the carpet gets rumbled.

It has also been observed that cotton thread has been started to use in the çözgü knot system after the 18th century. The usage of this thread is more wide-spread nowadays. Since the strength of the carpet depends on the çözgü knots it can be concluded that the usage of cotton thread will definitely affect the strength of the carpet.

Knots are a very important factor in determining the quality or a carpet.

In the ancient carpets there were 3x4 or 4x4 knots in each cm².

After the weaving of the carpet is finished it goes through a washing phase. Washing is important inthe sense that the colors turn out to be more livelier and brighter at the end.

For this process the carpet is treated with 2 kgr. of is put into 180-220 liters of water. This solution is obsorbed by the fluffy partof the carpet. This solution affects the dye, especially synthetic dye. So when the carpet is tre ted with this solution the colors mix into each other. In the second phase the hydrosulphate solution is applied to the carpet. The solution is obtained by mixing half a cup of hydrosulphate into a basin full of water. The water in the basin has to be quite hot it should even be at the boiling point. The hydrosulphate rinses the colors that have previously been mixed together. After this the carpet is washed with plenty of water. Then it is squeezed in a roller pin until there is no more water in the fulffy part Next the carpet is coated with a mixture made of chlor and slaked lime. The duty of the slaked lime is to fix colors that have been cleaned.

CARPETMAKING REGIONS IN TURKEY

EDİRNE

SİNO

İSTANBUL

HEREKE

MARMARA

İZMİT

BANDIRMA

MANYAS

ÇANAKKALE

BURSA

Kızılırmak

EZİNE

SINDIRGI-YAĞCIBEDİR

ANKARA

BERGAMA

BALIKESİR

KIRŞEHİR

GÖRDES

MUĞ

Gediz

AKHİSAR

UŞAK

İZMİR

KULA

ÇAL

AYDIN

AKSARAY

E DENİZİ

KONYA

NİĞD

GEAN SEA

TAŞPINAR

MİLAS

ISPARTA

KARAPINAR

MUĞLA

DÖŞEMEALTI

ANTALYA

AKDENİZ

MEDITERRANEAN

AKHİSAR

A district of Manisa.

Carpets woven there are the prayer-rug types with double bordures and singlestaired niches. There is no 'ayetlik' (place to read verse) or no 'ayaklık' (pedal). From the top of these traingular niches a chandelier hangs down. In the 'kilim' parts there are round or oval 'evil-eye charmas'. (These are seen inthe Bergama carpets as well). The same elements are seen in the 'etlik' part as tassels.

The colors used are red, white, blue, dark-blue, yellow, green and brown.

Halı-seccade (20th Cent.)
1.30x1.71 m. Wool.

ANTALYA - DÖŞEMEALTI

Döşemealtı is a region to the north-west of Antalya made up of 23 villages. The Kovanlık and Aşağıoba villages can be considered the centers of carp eting.

In the Döşemealtı region there are seven kinds of base compositions:

1) Halelli
2) Toplu
3) Kocasulu
4) Dallı
5) Mihraplı
6) Akrepli
7) Terazi Toplu

Among these, only the ones called 'Halelli' have no corner design. All the others are carpets which can be seen very often in Döşemealtı; with two niches and corner designs.

It is uhderstood that the Halelli carpet is the type which has the oldest traditional composition. The base design is composed of the Arabic Hand Fold, yantır, şıngır and balls of leaves. The attention is not focused on one spot but the composition is spread balancedly and it seems as if the design is going to continue even after the bordures. This reflects, as mentioned before 'The Principle of Eternity'.

Other than these seven other kinds of base designs which seem to be very old have been found recently. These indicate that there must have been more base compositions.

a) The base has two niches. The inner and outer corners of the niches are folded. There are two vertical 'fold lines'. The other parts are rectangles which are made of the 'Kocasu' or 'el' (hand) designs. In between there are şıngır designs. The triangular empty spaces at the top are filled with kettles and balls but the bottom is only filled with balls.

b) The base design has double and staired niches. The corneres are filled with 'braneching lanyard' of fours or fives. The base is filled large balls which are in harmony with the niche triangles on both sides.

c) The pase is very distinctive. Right in the middle, as if dividing the base into two there are four Arabic designs at the sides surrounded by a row of 'tutmaç' balls. On the longer sides one, on the shorter, two rows of 'tutmaç' balls are in between. And these make up adjacent hexagons which are filled with eight cornered stars.

Among the traditional and characteristic bordures of Döşemealtı are 'Deve Suyu', 'Tutmaç Suyu', and 'Bulanık'. The designs which make up the 'Deve Suyu look like a bird at first sight. But actually it is inspired after the camel and it has a very pretty style. We can see a similar design on the fifteenth century Bergama carpet called 'Marby'. The similar designs are also on the multi-colored sacks of the Döşemealtı-Kovanlık region. It can be figured that the designs on the sacks were later put on the carpets.

In the Döşemealtı region the colors which used were: red, pistachio green, dark green, dark brown, green, camel hair, light and dark blue, yellow orange, dried rose, violet and white.

In the modern ones there are decrease and change in colors. The colors are dark blue, indigo, purple, red, dark green, d ark brown and white.

Both the antique and modern Döşemealtı carpets are smaal in size.

Back page, left:
Antalya-Döşemealtı (20th Cent.)
1.26x1.83 m. Wool
3x4 knots per cm2.

Back page, right:
Döşemealtı (19th Cent.)
1.28x1.57 m. Wool
3x3 knots per cm2.

Antalya-Döşemealtı (20th Cent.) 0.80x1.20 m. Wool. 3x4 knots per cm2.

45

AVANOS

It's a district of Nevşehir and it is to the north-east of Nevşehir.

The carpet-type is usually the prayer-rug type. The prayer-rugs have single and staired niches. Some have the 'ayetlik' (place to read verse). Their most distinctive characteristics are double and teethed bordures. These are three pieces within each other and made of floral designs.

Red, yellow, and green are the main colors. Light blue is used to.

Avanos-Prayer rug (20th Cent.)
1.24x1.71 m. Wool
4x4 knots per cm².

Avanos-divanlık (20th Cent.) ▷
1.25x1.92 m. Wool
4x4 knots per cm².

BANDIRMA

It's a district of Balıkesir. It is to the west of Balıkesir and at the end-point of Bandırma bay.

Usually prayer-rugs are woven. The prayer-rugs have pedals and verse reading places so the base of the niches are narrow.

The bordures occupy more space. The distinctive characteristic of these carpets are that the top of the niches there is no triangle but instead just a round oval head (Just like gravestones). From the top of the niche towards the bottom, hangs a chandelier. The niche is ornamented with delicate oil-lamps. At the top and bottom of the oil-lamps there are ram horns and floral ornamentations.

The colors are: yellow, red, white, different tones of brown, green, beige.

Bandırma-Prayer rug (20th Cent.)
1.31x1.80 m. Wool
4x5 knots per cm².

◁ Avanos-Kandilli (20th Cent.) 1.05x1.92 m. Wool 4x4 knots per cm².

BERGAMA

Adistrict of Izmir and to the north of Izmir.

The three most important weaving centers of the Bergama region are Yağcıbedir, Yuntdağı and Kozak.

The most important traditional characteristic of these carpets are that the base compositions are made of geometrical divisions.The designs,being in harmony with the base design are geometrical, too. The colors are red, orange, blue, yellow, green and white.

Yağcıbedir is in the west of Bergama. The Kocaoba village, where a great deal of weaving is done, can be regarded as the center.

Nowadays the most distinctive prayer-rug type is the one called 'Oba namazlığı' (Tent prayer-rug). The more antique ones are almost square in shape. The colors are white, red and dark-blue or purple, white and dark-blue.

Yuntdağı is to the south of Bergama and it seems more attached to its traditions. The 'Tabaklı' (plated) rug, sets a good example to this. THe base is divided into eight squares. The diddors are vertically two, and horizontally four. The horizontal dividors are considered as the main ones. So the carpet is called 'Dört tabaklı' (four plated). Each division on the base is called 'plate'.

The second type of carpet in the Yuntdağı region is the seccade (Prayer-Rug). It is called 'Ibrikli' (kettled). The wide bordure is the 'Deve Tabanı' (Colt's foot)The rug has a double and staired niche. And teh niche triangles are lenghtened with ram horns and the corners are filled with kettles surrounded by rectangular frames. ,

Kozak is to the north of Bergama. In the Yukarıbey, Çamavlu, Terzihaliller, Yukarıcuma and Aşağıcuma villages weaving is very popular as well.

Back page, left:
kız Bergama (19th Cent.)
1.08x1.37 m. Wool
Back page right:
Bergama-Yağcıbedir (20th Cent.)
1.15x1.28 m. Wool
4x5 knots per cm².

Yuntdağ-Prayer rug (19th Cent.)▽
1.05x1.82 m. Wool
3x4 knots per cm².

ÇAL

It is a district of Denizli and it is to the north of Denizli.

Usually rug typed carpets are woven. The rugs can either have single or double niches, and the niches are staired. There are no ayaklık (pedal) or ayetlik (verse reading parts) The base of the niches are ornamented with different designs. In the modern ones the niches can be woven without any ornamentation.

Red, white, orange, light and dark brown, violet and purple are among the colors which are used.

Çal (20th Cent.)
1.09x1.69 m. Wool
5x4 knots per cm².

Çal (19th Cent.) ▷
1.15x1.67 m. Wool
3x4 knots per cm².

ÇANAKKALE

There are tassels hanging from the etlik part of the carpet just like in the Akhisar carpet but these are less frequent. The carpets show a nomad characteristic. The wide bordures are usually like the 'Tumaç Suyu' bordure of Döşemealtı region. The narrow bordure is the one called 'Sığır Sidiği' (Bull's urine). The colors are striking. They are red, white, blue or dark blue, orange and yellow. The designs are geometrical.

Çanakkale (20th Cent.)
1.35x2.05 m. Wool
3x3 knots per cm².

DAZKIRI

The antique rugs are small in size and almost square in shape. They can have single or double niches and they also have corner designs. As the corner design the 'Heybe Suyu' (Sack pattern) of the Döşemealtı region is used. The 'Turunçlu-Süpürgeli Göl' (Lime-Broom lake) design which resembles the designs of Milas is used very often for the base. Some have pedals and verse reading places. In the wide bordures, sometimes, designs which resemble the Gördes designs are used. Today in Dazkırı there are four main types of carpet compositions and these are: 1) Patterned Lyric Poemed 2) Big poemed floor carpets, 3) Wheeled floor carpet and 4) Chandeliered. The first one is closer to the characteristic and tradition of Dazkırı.

The colors used are red, white, dark green, blue, yellow and brown.

Dazkırı (19th Cent.)
1.47x2.21 m. Wool
3x4 knots per cm².

EZİNE

It is a district of Çanakkale and it is to the south-west of Çanakkale. The carpets resemble very much the ones of Çanakkale and they are of nomad characteristic. Rugs in small sizes are woven. The rugs have especially two or three bordures. The wide bordures are made of big and double leaves and which make up zigzags or big lozenge-shaped patterns which are joined together or of big hexagon balls.

The base is made of big geometrical designs.

The colors used are red, white, yellow, blue and dark blue.

Ezine-Prayer rug (20th Cent.)
0.97x1.32 m. Wool
3x3 knots per cm².

Ezine (20th Cent.) ▷
1.17x1.80 m. Wool
3x3 knots per cm².

EAST ANATOLIA

In carpeting, Karks can be shown as representative for this region. They show the same characteristics as the caucasian carpets.

The base designs are geometrical and patterned. The big geometric patterns catch the attention very easily. The colors used are strong red, dark blue, blue and white. Other than these green and yellow are among the colors used.

Kars-Caucasian (19th Cent.)
1.46x2.00 m. Wool.
4x4 knots per cm².

back page:
Elazığ-Maden (20th Cent.)
1.24x2.01 m.
4x4 knots per cm².
Top, right:
Caucasian (20th Cent.)
1.28x1.81 m. Wool.
3x3 knots per cm².

Bottom, right:
Caucasian (20th Cent.)
1.267x1.76 m. Wool.
3x3 knots per cm².

◁ Kars-Caucasian (19th Cent.) 1.12x2.06 m., 3x4 knots per cm², wool.

FETHİYE

It is a district of Muğla and it is to the south-east of Muğla.

The bases are usually ornamented with rose-leaf and branches which make up a naturalistic bunch. The carpets are single niched and staired and the bases are again filled with rose bouquets. The carpets with medaillon designs show the same characteristic.

The Megris are somewhat different and of nomad origin. The long and narrow rectangular base has turned into an octagon and is double niched. The base is filled with symetrical branches from whose ends stars hang down.

The colors are red, white, yellow, orange and dark blue.

Megri-Prayer rug (20th Cent.)
1.02x1.71 m. Wool.
3x4 knots per cm2.

GÖRDES

It is a district of Manisa and it is to the north-east of Manisa.

Almost all Gördes carpets are rug types. There are four main types a) Çubuklu, b) Marpuçlu, c) Ibrikli and d) Kız Gördes. Except for the Kız Gördes all the others are single niched. The Ibriklis can even be without any niches. The Çubuklu (sticked) Gördes carpets take their names after the seven narrow and thin bordures. The number can sometimes be less. On the inner or outer sides of the thin bordures there can be one wide bordure.

Kız (girl) Gördes carpets have almost all narrow bases and the dominant color is a sweet red which is almost purple. Dark blue, yellow and green are also colors which are used for the base. Bu it can be observed that after the eighteenth century the color has turned into a biting pink and the yarn used has turned into cotton. It can also be seen that this pink coloris not only used in the base part but that it ison the whole of the carpet. Light blue and tones of brown are among the colors which are used.

Kız Gördes (18th Cent.)
1.32x2.17 m. Wool.
3x4 knots per cm².

Ürgüp (20th Cent.) 1.20x1.80 m. Wool 3x4 knots per cm². ▷

HEREKE

It is between Izmit-Gebze, in Kocaeli.
Although sometimes carpets in big sizes can be seen the commonly woven carpets are rather small in size. The reason for this is that, eventhough wool is used, silk is more often used. One one of the top corners of the carpet usually the word 'Hereke' is seen. The designs are round and circled branchleaves which are naturalistic ornamentation examples. The characteristic is influences by Persian carpets.

Hereke (20th Cent.)
1.21x2.15 m. Silk
12x12 knots per cm²

ISPARTA

It is in the Lake Region and it is a city for its roses.

The starting of carpeting in Isparta carpet is that the designs and patterns are made of circled branch-leaves of roses and several other flowers and that they are in a naturalistic fashion.

Eventhough these designs used to be much more disiplinized at earlier carpets, during the last years this situation has changed a great deal. It has changed so much that sometimes the bordures have been totally excluded and that carpeting has transformed itself into painting. This shows us that the Isparta carpet has to save itself somehow.

Machine yarn is used in carpets and the knot type is 'Sine' (persian)

Isparta-Taban (20th Cent.)
1.20x2.15 m. Wool, cotton.
3x3 knots per cm².

KARAPINAR

It is a district of Konya and it is to the east of Konya between Konya and Ereğli.

Both geometrical and floral designs and patterns are used. The former remind us of the Anatolia-Caucasia or ancient Bergama designs. As an example we can give the three big adjacent octagons which are used for the base. The octagons are filled with eight cornered stars. The colors used are red, dirty yellow, light yellow, purple and violet.

The prayer rugs have single and staired niches. The bottom part of the niches are largely zigzagged and the sides have triangular recesses. Both the niche and the corners are ornamented. The colors used are red, white, purple, orange, green, light blue and dark brown.

Karapınar-Prayer rug (20th Cent.)
1.24x1.63 m. Wool.
3x4 knots per cm².

Karapınar-Yatak (19 th. Cent.) ▷
1.24x1.87 m. Wool.
3x4 knots per cm².

KIRŞEHİR

The anciant Kırşehir carpets had single and staired niches, the niches having double lines, pedals and verse reading places. The typical wide bordure is like the one seen in (III.   ). Together with the wide bordure sticked bordures are used as well. The wide bordures are also seen in the corner spaces and the pedals. The inner of the top, left and right of the base is filled with large zigzags. The colors used are red, blue, yellow, dirty green and white.

Kırşehir-Prayer rug (20th Cent.)
1.17x1.70 m. Wool.
4x4 knots per cm².

Kırşehir (19th Cent.) ▷
1.09x1.56 m. Wool.
4x4 knots per cm².

KULA

It is a district of Manisa and it is to the east of Manisa between Manisa and Uşak.

The most striking characteristic of the ancient Kula carpet is that the bordures are very thin, in other words sticked like the Gördes ones and that the dominant coloris apricot yellow. But wide bordures are used too and the mostly used design are the styled branch-leaf-flowers

They can have either single or double niches.

The base is ornamented with small dots or floral designs, in a very simple fashion.

The prayer-rugs whose base is made up of the 'House and Tree' designs are called 'Mezarlıklı Kula' (Kula with graveyards).

Colors used, other than apricot yellow, are yellow, red, blue, tones of brown white and green.

Kula-Prayer rug (18th Cent.)
1.24x1.97 m. Wool.
4x4 knots per cm².

Kula-Graveyard (20th Cent.) ▷
1.26x1.87 m. Wool
4x4 knots per cm².

LADİK

It is a carpeting center of Konya and it is between Konya and Akşehir.

The ancient Ladik Prayer-rugs usually have one niche and three bordures. They are usually not staired. In the pedal and verse-reading parts tulips and poppys, that are in proper rows, can be seen.

The wide bordures are made of either big tulips with big ball-like flowers inbetween or of a narrow rectangle which is made of again, round flowers placed among spearheads. And there are also wide bordures made of geometrical figures.

The niche bases are very simple and the dominant colors are dars blue and purple. Other colors used are red, yellow and green.

The more modern ones have niches with stairs. The ornamentation designs are usually floral.

Ladik-Prayer rug (Late 19th Cent.)
1.10x1.51 m. Wool.
3x4 knots per cm².

Ladik-Prayer rug (19th Cent.) ▷
1.10x1.65 m. Wool
4x4 knots per cm².

MİLAS

It is a district of Muğla and it is to the west of Muğla and between Söke and Bodrum.

Like all the other Milas carpets, its prayer-rugs have very wide bordures and the base is a narrow rectangle.

The niche of the prayer-rug looks like a lozenge because of two triangles that go into the niche from the two top sides These are called'Mihrabın cepleri' (the packets of the niche). The flowers that come out of the two sides of the niche are called 'Mihrabın Elleri' (the hands of the niche). These are the most important characteristics of the Milas prayer-rugs. There are no pedals or verse reading parts. In some of the prayer rugs we san see that some things hang down the sides of the niches. These are called 'Serpinti' or 'Arpacık'. Again, from the sides of the niche, triangular designs in threes, hang down. These are called 'Terazi' (scale)

Although the ornamentation designs are usually floral, sometimes totally geometrical figures can be seen too. The colors usedare sweet and bright red, apricot yellow, white, green, blue and brown. The colors used to be brighter in the ancient carpets whereas they are not that striking nowadays.

Milas-Prayer rug (20th Cent.) ▽
1.24x1.74 m. Wool.
3x4 knots per cm².

Milas-Prayer rug (20th Cent.) ▷
1.18x1.72 m. Wool
3x3 knots per cm².

MUCUR

It is a district of Kırşehir and it is to the south-west of Kırşehir.

The most commonly woven carp et type is the Prayer-rug. They can have either single or double niches and these have either only verse reading places or in addition the pedal too. Among the most distinctive characteristics are the wide bordures made up of rows of stylistic leaves. The other bordures contain geometrical figures as well. Stylistic kettles are among the designs used. The niche bases are often plain and red in color. The modern carpets have purple as their base-color.

The colors used are red, blue, yellow, green, purple and white.

Mucur-Prayer rug (Late 19th Cent.)
1.02x1.64 m. Wool
3x3 knots per cm².

Mucur Prayer rug (20th Cent.) ▷
1.20x1.89 m., wool.
3x3 knots per cm²

SINDIRGI - YAGCIBEDİR

It is a district of Balıkesir and to the south-east of Balıkesir.

The carpets woven are usually prayer-rugs. The niches are double and staired.

Although the designs are usually geometrical and floral, sometimes very fine and delicate human and animal figures can be seen. Again stylistic kettles are among the designs that are used. All designs are expressed in geometric patterns. Both the niche base and the triangular spaces are ornamented.

The colors used are pale red, red, white, dark blue and royal blue.

Yağcıbedir-Prayer rug
(20th Cent.)
1.15x1.42 m., wool.
5x5 knots per cm².

Sındırgı-Yağcıbedir ▷
(20th Cent.)
1.21x1.62 m. Wool.
4x5 knots per cm².

SİVAS

Its prayer-rugs are staired and they have single niches. The base of the niche and the triangular spaces have floral ornamentation.

Some may have verse reading places. Although usually the 'Gemi Suyu' (ship pattern) bordure of the Milas region is used for the wide bordures, sometimes bordures which remind us of the wide bordures of the Mucur region, are used.

The colors used are red, orange, light yellow, dark brown and red.

Sivas-Mihraplı, (19th Cent.)
1.22x1.68 m. Wool
4x5 knots per cm2.
Back page:
Sivas-Zara (Late 19th Cent.)

Yağcıbedir (20th Cent.) 1.20x1.76 m.Wool. 5x5 knots per cm2.

87

TAŞPINAR

It is a weaving center that belongs to Niğde and it is to the north-west of Niğde.

Prayer-rug types of carpets are woven. The rugs can either have single or double niches. The niches are staired. There are big middle compositions in the double niches and the corners are ornamented.

The ornamentations are floral.

In the wide bordures, bordures which resemble the ones of Mucur are used.

In some rugs we can see small flowers that hang down to the bottom part from the inner part of the inner bordure.

The colors used are red, white, light yellow, indigo, dried rose, green and dark blue.

Taşpınar-Prayer rug (20th Cent.)
1.47x2.34 m. Wool.
3x4 knots per cm².

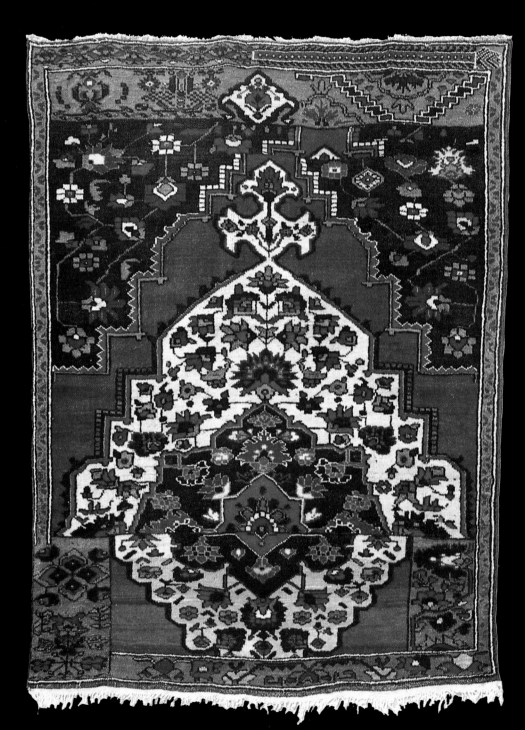

UŞAK

It is a very old weaving center.

In the ancient Uşak carpets mainly, six different compositions can be seen. a) Madalyonle (medailloned), b) Yıldızlı (starred), c) Kuşlu (birded), d) Post motifli (furred), e) Çiçekli (flowered), f) Çin motifi (Chinese designs). Exlanations about these have been given previously.

These carpets usually have four bordures. The first and the third are made of stylistic flowers. As in the fourth bordure resembles the 'Bulanık' (turbid) bordure of the Antalya-Döşemealtı region. The wide bordure is rather different. It is made of big stylistic leaves and geometrical figures with comb like figures on either side. In the base there is a big equilateral square, as the middle composition. The corners are ornamented with very large branch-leaves and flowers.

Uşak-Floral (18th Cent.)
1.00x1.64m., wool.
3x4 knots per cm2,

◁ Taşpınar-Vagire (20th Cent.) 1.20x1.65 m., 4x4 knots per cm2, wool.

91

YAHYALI

It is a district of Kayseri and it is to the south of Kayseri.

Prayer - rug type carpets are woven. The rugs have pedals and verse reading places. In some rugs, the two triangles of a hexagon make the niche of the rug. The base and spaces of the niche is ornamented. In some niche bases there are big middle designs which resemble medaillons.

The colors are usually dark. Red, dark blue, white and brown are the main colors.

Yahyalı-Zile (20th Cent.)
0.87x1.28m., wool.
3x4 knots per cm2,

Yahyalı (20th Cent.) ▷
1.21x1.61m, wool.
4x5 knots per cm2,

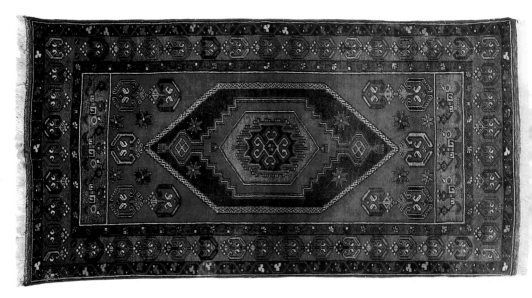

Yahyalı (20th Cent.) 1.34x1.86m., 4x4 knots per cm² wool.

TAŞKALE

Its former name being 'Kızıllı', it is a village of Konya-Karaman.

Carpets woven are usually prayer-rugs. But sometimes bed-rugs are woven too. The bed-rugs are also in the prayer-rug style.

The rugs have double niches and they are staired with big hexagonic middle designs. Naturalistic designs don't take place very much.

In these type of rugs the head and bottom parts are definitely distinguished. This distinction is made in three ways:

1) At the head partof the rug there are six patterns whereas at the bottom part there are only five.

2) From the head corner designs down to the bottom part one 'Çömçe' design hangs down to the bottom.

3) The corner designs at the head part are different from those at the bottom.

The colors used are black, white, red, dark brown, yellow, violet and green.

MANYAS

It is to the north of Balıkesir.

The carpets show a nomad characteris-tic and they are small in size.

The base is filled with big octagons that are ornamented with eight cornered stars. The color used are red, green, blue, light and dark yellow and white.

BIBLIOGRAPHY

Abdülkadir İnan, Tarihte ve Bugün Şamanizma-Materyaller ve Araştırmalar , Türk Tarih Kurumu Yayınlarından VII.

Ahmet Günindi. Türk El Dokusu Halıcılığı.

Ali Rızı Yalman Yalgın, Canupta Türkmen Oymakları II, Kültür Bakanlığı, Yayınları: 256, Kültür Eserleri: 14, Milli Eğitim Basımevi, İstanbul, 1977.

Celâl Esat Arseven, Türk Sanatı, Yayınevi, 1970.

Doç. Dr. M. Kemal Özergin, Halı, Türk Folklor Araştırmaları.

Gn. Kâzım Dirik, Eski ve Yeni Türk Halıcılığı ve Cihan Halı Tipleri Panoraması.

Heinrich Glück, Türk Sanatı (Eski Türk Sanatı ve Avrupa'ya Etkisi), Türkiye İş Bankası Yayınları.

İslâm Ansiklopedisi, Milli Eğitim Basımevi, 1964.

J. Strzygowski, Türkler ve Ortaasya Sanatı, (Türk Sanatı ve Avrupa'ya Etkisi).

Kenan Özbel, El Sanatları XI, Anadolu Halı Seccadeleri. Kılavuz Kitaplar XXII.

Kurt Erdman, 15. Asır Türk Halısı (Türkçesi: H.Taner), İstanbul Üniversitesi Edebiyat Fakültesi Yayınları: 715.

Kurt Erdman, Seven Hunred Years of Oriental Carpets, London, Faber And limited 1970.

Kurt Zipper, Türk Halıcıları, Sanat Dünyamız, Yapı ve Kredi Bankasının bir Kültür Hizmeti.

Macide Gönül, Eski Dokumacılık ve Yurdumuzdaki Gelişimi II, Araştırmaları.

Macide Gönül, Türk Halı ve Kilimlerinden yapılan Eşyalar, Türk Folklor Araştırmaları.

Melek Celâl, Türk İşlemeleri.

Naci Eren, Antalya Bölgesinde Bitkisel Boyacılık, Türk Etnografya Dergisi.

Naci Eren, Antalya-Döşemealtı Eski ve Yeni Halıları, Türk Etnografya Dergisi.

Nejat Diyarbekirli, Hun Sanatı, Milli Eğitim Bakanlığı Kültür Yayınları.

Nurettin Yatman, Türk Kumaşları, Ankara Halkevi Neşriyatı.

Oktay Aslanapa-Yusuf Durul, Selçuk Halıları (Başlangıcından 16. yüzyıl ortalarına Kadar), Akbank'ın Bir Kültür Hizmeti. Ak Yayınları.

Prof.Dr. Bahaeddin Ögel, Türk Kültür Tarihine Giriş III, Kültür Bakanlığı Yayınları: 244.

Şerare Yetkin, Türk Halı Sanatı, İş Bankası Kültür Yayınları:

Tevfik Hacıhamdioğlu, Alanya Folkloru, Namal Matbaası,

Türk Ansiklopedisi, Milli Eğitim Basımevi, Ankara.

Yusuf Durul, El Dokuma Halıcılığının İçinde Bulunduğu Sorunlar ve Çözüm Yolları, 1979 Sümerbank Genel Müdürlüğü Türk El Dokuma Halıcılığı Semineri Teksir Notları.

PERGAMON

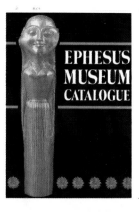

- **ENGLISH**
  ISBN 975-7487-01-5
- **GERMAN**
  ISBN 975-7487-02-3
- **FRENCH**
  ISBN 975-7487-04-X
- **ITALIAN**
  ISBN 975-7487-03-1
- **SPANISH**
  ISBN 975-7487-06-0
- **DUTCH**
  ISBN 975-7487-24-4
- **GREEK**
  ISBN 975-7487-05-8

EPHESUS

- **ENGLISH**
  ISBN 975-7487-07-4
- **GERMAN**
  ISBN 975-7487-08-2
- **FRENCH**
  ISBN 975-7487-10-4
- **ITALIAN**
  ISBN 975-7487-09-0
- **SPANISH**
  ISBN 975-7487-11-2
- **DUTCH**
  ISBN 975-7487-12-0
- **JAPAN**
  ISBN 975-7487-18-X

EPHESUS MUSEUM CATALOGUE

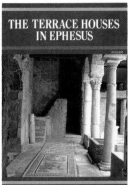

89-34 Y. 0037-10

- **ENGLISH**
- **GERMAN**
- **FRENCH**

PAMUKKALE HIERAPOLIS

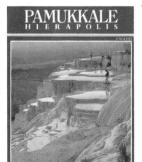

- **ENGLISH**
  ISBN 975-7487-00-7
- **GERMAN**
  ISBN 975-7487-23-6
- **FRENCH**
  ISBN 975-7487-22-8
- **ITALIAN**
  ISBN 975-7487-21-X
- **SPANISH**
  ISBN 975-7487-19-8
- **DUTCH**
  ISBN 975-7487-20-1

THE TERRACE HOUSES IN EPHESUS

88-34 Y.0037-6

- **ENGLISH**
- **GERMAN**
- **FRENCH**

TURKISH HANDMADE CARPETS

- **ENGLISH**
  ISBN 975-7487-26-0
- **GERMAN**
  ISBN 975-7487-25-2
- **FRENCH**
  ISBN 975-7487-29-5
- **ITALIAN**
  ISBN 975-7487-28-7
- **JAPAN**
  ISBN 975-7487-27-9

CAPPADOCIA

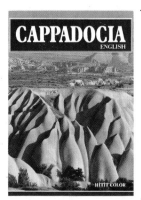

- **ENGLISH**
  ISBN 975-7487-14-7
- **GERMAN**
  ISBN 975-7487-13-9
- **FRENCH**
  ISBN 975-7487-17-1
- **ITALIAN**
  ISBN 975-7487-16-3
- **SPANISH**
  ISBN 975-7487-16-3

With Compliments

 HİTİT COLOR